Extant

poems by Jenny L. Davis

Michigan State University Press
East Lansing, Michigan 48823-5245

Library of Congress Cataloging-in-Publication Data is available
ISBN 978-1-61186-573-8 (paper)
ISBN 978-1-60917-827-7 (PDF)
ISBN 978-1-62895-577-4 (ePub)

Cover by Erin Kirk.
Artwork by Jenny L. Davis.

Visit Michigan State University Press at *www.msupress.org*

EXTANT

AMERICAN INDIAN STUDIES SERIES

Jill Doerfler, *Series Editor*

A full list of titles in this series is provided in the back of this book.

If ever we are constrained to lift the hatchet against any tribe, we will never lay it down till that tribe is exterminated, or driven beyond the Missisipi [sic]: adjuring them therefore, if they wish to remain on the land which covers the bones of their fathers, to keep the peace with a people who ask their friendship without needing it, who wish to avoid war without fearing it. In war they will kill some of us; we shall destroy all of them.

—Thomas Jefferson to Henry Dearborn, August 28, 1807

I call the soldier
with a tired arm
who didn't cut deeply enough
into my great-grandfather's chest to kill clean.
I return your axehead
oiled and sharpened
wield it against others with equal skill.

—from "Giveaway," Kim Shuck, 2005

Contents

EXTANT

Apocalypse Journals

It is the 21st day of the 9th month
of the 524th year of the apocalypse,
and the tobacco plant is blooming.
As I poured water into soil,
I leaned forward to ask
the pale pink petals,
How can you flower
in all this chaos?

She didn't hesitate
to answer, *My child,*
it is the only time
to bloom,
each season is dangerous
in its own ways,
and if you
hold your breath
until it's safe
you will suffocate.
It is always the apocalypse.

Public/Science

Q: "Are Native Americans Extinct?" (Quora)

A:

extant Native American
populations
are
low
but
consistent

—*American Journal of Physical Anthropology*, 2008

Taxonomy of the Difficult World

Endangered

Almost gone! Come see and hear us before it's too late! If you're lucky you might get to touch one of us. Be careful, some of us bite.

Some species manage to be simultaneously endangered in their original lands and invasive everywhere else. The routes that carried them from one part of the world to another are no longer available for a return trip.

> See brushtail possum, see Puerto Rican coquí

Extant

My apologies for not
already being dead
I know it is
uncomfortable
for both of us,

especially you.

> See Native American, see Taino, see Tasmanian, see Palestinian

Extinct

Declarations of our extinction may have been exaggerated.

> See Lazarus species

Lazarus species

It appears some of us have taken the game of "hide and seek" too seriously and some people are very bad at looking. The ivory-billed woodpecker has been holding out for 80 years. Then, *Boo! Got ya! Your turn to hide!*

> See black-footed ferret, see Sinixt Nation, see Myaamia, Tunica, and Wampanoag Languages

Imilhlha means to be wild, to be afraid

In the 10th century, *dēor* (deer)
could refer to any
manner of wild animal

European maps
from that time
were full of
monsters

combinations of
humans and lions
with wings, fins, and scales
fill the areas of
deep water

and the Americas are
illustrated with trees
and beasts of the woods
on two and four legs

Make no mistake
this is still unsettled territory
Here there be Deer and Savages

Where do we see it from

for AB

Rich's positionality theorem contends
    that the universe is only ever partially observable
    that what is knowable is relative to the position of the observer
to *this* place, *this* time,
to the gravitational pull of history engraved in flesh and memory
    that *this* is the place where we met
is as significant as any battle, any bloodshed that
might have played out here
    that we share the small distinctions of what we can and cannot see
not because our view is universal
but because the murmuration of our field reports
is a way of knowing vastness
and each other

native American dogs (or, The Difference a Single Capital Letter Makes)

Q: Do you have to be related or specifically native American to become a werewolf? (Reddit)

A: Dogs colonized the Americas and were widespread by the time Europeans arrived late in the 15th century.

This striking difference between ancient and modern dogs suggests that very little of the extant population trace back to the native American population.

However, we caution that the average native American in the extant population could be different if dogs contributed offspring

—*BMC Evolutionary Biology*, 2011

Over a Barrel

If the only words you have are
bullets
then speak

If your voice can only be heard
coming from the mouth of a gun
let it sound

Every time I leave the house
I prepare myself
to listen

Defense Mechanisms

The soft bodies
of earthworms
mean that their presence
in the fossil record
is almost non-existent
isn't it fascinating
that in 209 million years
they have never evolved
antlers, barbs, bristles, carapaces, casings, endoskeletons, exoskeletons,
fangs, fur, hair, hooves, horns, hulls, husks, lamellas, manes, nails, peltidia,
pelts, pincers, plastrons, plates, prongs, quills, rachis, scales, shells,
snares, spines, spurs, squamae, stingers, talons, teeth, thoraces, tines, toxins,
tusks, venom, whiskers, wings, or wool
yet they can be found
on every continent
on the planet
steadfastly surviving
through radical
vulnerability

Tisquantum 2025

Like some titan cursed
by the gods, I have been
teaching these late
arrivals how to grow without destroying
    how to live without killing
    how to be a decent guest
for over four hundred
years. Every day, this same
task repeats itself from
the beginning. Every day
they slay me in the process.
Their eagle dines on my
organs and the words from
my mouth are merely
the echoes of those around
me. Every day it's still the
goddamn *Mayflower*.

Lessons from Cicada

Humans born
in the year of the cicada
are nearing adulthood
before the two
groups meet again

To live they must peel off
old bodies,
perfect under the ground
but suddenly
too tight against wings
surging to unfurl

They come prepared
to feed the whole forest
offering a feast
of their own flesh until
Raccoon, Cardinal, and Turtle
are too sated to move

Their songs ring
through the trees,
calling the beat for dances
between branches
and the mating those flights draw

In death they offer feast again
as their numbers
blanket the forest ground
and tree rings mark
their offering

An existence filled with
a flight,
a fuck,
a song,
and a feast is enough
for a beautiful life cycle

We were all born
in a year of the cicada

Life and Limb

The octopus eats its own leg.
—Takashi Murakami

Sometimes I
think of myself as
an octopus working
without an arm. But a shell's
reflection just showed
me I'm the severed limb
still feeling along
for delicious things to
feed a body no longer
connected to me.
You'll forgive me
if I don't remember
(in my headless state)
how long it's been
since I was attached to
anything that sustained me
if I pulled the guillotine
chord myself or waited
while someone else did the job.
Bodies sometimes grow
new appendages
but severed limbs don't
create new heads
can't reattach to a viable
beating heart. But what else
is there to do but feel around
in this alcove for food. To
keep my head down (as it were).

Who knows maybe I'll be the first
to make a new home
out of nothing.

Repatriation Goddam

after Nina Simone
on the passing of revisions to the Native American
Graves Protection and Repatriation Act
January 12, 2024

We don't belong here
They don't belong here
It's been so long since they've heard a prayer
Don't tell me
I tell you
Me and my people just about due
I've been there so I know
They keep on saying "Go slow!"
But that's just the trouble
"Do it slow"
Finish the inventories
"Do it slow"
Consult with our Nations
"Do it slow"
You're just vindictive
"Do it slow"
You don't understand this
"Do it slow"
The thinking's crazy
"Do it slow"
Where are we going
What are we doing
I don't know
I don't know
Just try to do your very best
Stand up be counted with all the rest
For everybody knows about repatriation goddam

Public/Science

Q: "Natives? They still exist?" (Reddit)

A: a very small set of authors to claim to represent minority extant populations,

—Reason given by editorial staff of *Science* for not sending an article with Indigenous authors out for review, 2021

Refugium

found poem

Animals avoid
predator attack
in different
ways; some
carry defensive
structures to
reduce predation,

as a portable refugium.

The Gulf of America

on the executive order to rename the Gulf of Mexico
January 20, 2025

is the distance
between the slaver's whip
the calvary's rifle
the lynch mob's noose
the cop's bullets

and the people pretending
not to see the bodies
piled all around them

Sharp Knives Cut All Flesh

I was born a knife from
a long line of knives
sharp, strong, and capable
of cutting anything
everything
including myself

I was born a sheath from
a long line of sheaths
perfectly shaped to manage
the sharp edges
of others

I refuse the forms
handed down to me
every time fear tells me
to reach for the
hilt of myself or
to make a home for
someone else's anger
glorified as justifiable
but really just aimed at
the closest available target

I am too busy
reforging my own fury
into a garden trowel
the nib of a pen
a Band-Aid tin

to take on yours

Preferred Collector

Pulse

June 12, 2016

I wish I could say the target surprises me
but we learned decades ago
to leave those rainbow clubs in groups
we are more visible now
but that does not make us safe.
We have to die for you to see us
to acknowledge we have names and
there are more words for how we die
than the ways we live.

After the shooting I planted 50 tobacco
seeds and sang them lullabies by Madonna,
Selena, and Grace Jones, hummed
Shilombish holitopa ma as I buried them
in the dirt. If we have to bleed out for you to
see we are human, may our blood be the iron
that feeds each ceremonial leaf and flower

Songs of Resistance

Unbolt the door
and put the tea kettle on

Warm your voice for the
songs of resistance

Get the folding chairs
from the basement

Bake some bread for the travelers

Stoke the fire for those
that stay behind

Listen for the weavings of
Spider, Crow, Fox, and Rabbit

We'll need the tricksters
for this

Our alliances have
never been legal

They hold nonetheless

Mimesis

<table>
<tr><td>The driving desire</td><td>to stand out</td></tr>
<tr><td>is a privilege of</td><td>the majority</td></tr>
<tr><td>of living in categories</td><td>automatically</td></tr>
<tr><td>marked normal, ideal, and</td><td>default</td></tr>
<tr><td>the rest of us spend</td><td>our whole lives</td></tr>
<tr><td>generations even</td><td></td></tr>
<tr><td>developing strategies</td><td>to</td></tr>
<tr><td>blend in, avoid</td><td>unwanted attention</td></tr>
<tr><td>practicing the stillness of</td><td>our</td></tr>
<tr><td>background leaves</td><td></td></tr>
<tr><td>and contorting our</td><td>colors</td></tr>
<tr><td>to the patterns around us</td><td></td></tr>
<tr><td>the bird of paradise</td><td></td></tr>
<tr><td>blooming</td><td></td></tr>
<tr><td>against a sea of uniform</td><td></td></tr>
<tr><td>bermuda is</td><td>quickly cut</td></tr>
<tr><td>for ornamentation</td><td></td></tr>
</table>

Honor Song for Tulsa

on the 100-year anniversary of the Tulsa Massacre
May 31, 2021

The name *Tulsa* comes from the
Muskogee word *Tallasi*
meaning "old town"
but this place also holds names from
other languages
like the *Mingo* Valley
from Choctaw and Chickasaw when
Tulsa made a home for us
after ours was taken
and *Greenwood*—for the street
that marked a segregation line
and the thriving
then destruction of life
but we have other names too
for ceremony and for family
and for each of the ways we relate
to each other
to this place
names that remember
that these city streets are the fraternal twins
of rivers, birthed at the same mouth
and slowly finding
their own separate paths, together
names that hold space
for histories that textbooks and
AP exams have erased
in languages our grammar teachers
didn't even know existed

Tulsa is a relocation name
the name of a massacre
a place named *home*
by generations
who are still here
even after the etymologies of
our names have been forgotten

Public/Science

Q: "Where have all the native Americans gone?" (Twitter/X)

A: According to this hypothesis Native American populations are

extinct

—*PLOS One*, 2020

How the Oak Tree Came to Be

1. *itti' hakshish* (root)

Those early anthropologists
got it wrong—our traditional tales
weren't myths
They are prophesies

2. *naksish filammi'* (branch)

Do you know
the stories about how
Cedar and Willow
started out as humans
and became trees?
Even today they
continue to care
for us and we treat
them as kin

3. *nasi'* (acorn)

Oak trees are great
caregivers. Each acorn
is protected by a cupule
that acts as a packed lunch,
car seat, and knitted blanket
all-in-one. Ingenious. Darling
acorns, I can't pass up their roundness,
the stripes on *Quercus palustris*, the
absolute largeness of *Quercus macrocarpa*,

the way *Quercus rubra* fits perfectly
in my palm. I almost always have one
in my pocket, sometimes two

4. *nassapi' shokhalanchapi'* (red oak tree)

Our words are a way
of staying connected of
knowing ourselves
even in faraway places
of becoming
rooted

5. *itti hobak* (tree that won't bear fruit)

If I ever go missing
as Native women so often do
look for an oak tree
in an unexpected place
a canopy grown wide
on denim, adipose,
and ditch water

The River Has Missed You

The river has missed you

Can you blame her
for not being there when you finally returned?

for slipping away
into the air and clay
until only the baked imprints
of her limbs remain?

Sing her the swelling songs
Let her feel your weight as you dance above her

The river has missed you

Can you blame her
for rising to find you?

for so longing to feel the tickle of
your touch against the smooth rocks of her flesh
that she called out to the rains
and wind to carry her to you?

Sing her the lulling songs
Let her taste the sweet offerings of tobacco on your fingers

The river has missed you

She will forgive you
for waiting so long to visit again

for forgetting how it feels to finally exhale
and feel weightless
as she holds you in her arms

Listen to the healing songs
Let the water call you home

1 in 3 Indians

All of these statistics
are just an attempt
to map the containers of our lives
to make sense of the frayed
edges of our blankets and
the dust left coating the shelves
of our memorabilia
why the porcelain dog
has a missing ear or maybe
why we still keep it in pride of place
why our family albums are
not full of professional photos and
why some of the pictures show
signs of fire and flood
why some of the pages
have been ripped out all together

We Invite You

a choose your own adventure poem taken from actual emails

Dear Jenny,
Dr. Davis,
(only Native American on campus),
we can find online),

I am a(n) and I would like to include you in my
undergraduate student class assignment.
graduate student IRB-approved study.
postdoctoral researcher creative project.
faculty colleague linguistic analysis.
member of the public story.
journalist

For that I would need to collect your life history.
urine samples.
daily stress calendar.
Native language.
opinion about a recent film.
the current controversy.
domestic violence on reservations.
Indigenous fire practices.
government spending.
Columbus Day.
Indigenous foods.
mascots.
mascots.

mascots.

You will be named.
anonymized.
given a pseudonym.
assigned a number.
uncredited.

After the project is completed, your contribution will be used for future projects.
destroyed without archiving.
deposited in a database.
shared at conferences.
in publications.
with other researchers.

Quantum Entanglement Theory

on the first photo of quantum entanglement
July 13, 2019

I do not want to own you
or be your possession—
instead let's become entangled

form new constellations from
the missing particles
quantum theory says
are always still bound to us

be knitted together by
spider silk and conspiracies
of breath and skin and the
anticipation of
gravitational fields that touch
long before we do—
Milky Way waiting
for the coming of Andromeda

let us rest

My people
were no strangers to disasters—
fires, tornadoes, floods, and droughts
that scorch, bury, and reshape the earth
where we laid our ancestors to rest

So dig up the bundles
Test samples from the bones,
cloth, and clay—
for the good of science
toward that next publication
or a new grant

But don't pretend it's
what my ancestors would have wanted
We interred our loved ones
under our homes or within the great
mounded houses
knowing, when the time came,
they'd be returned
to the water, the mud,
and to the stars

Caudal Autotomy (Tail Loss as a Survival Strategy)

found poem

Many species of lizards
release their tail
when they want
to escape from

a predator.

The tail
then continues to wriggle
like a living creature,
which distracts
the predator
away from the lizard's

vulnerable body,

allowing it to escape
while the predator
is left holding
or trying to catch
the expendable

tail.

That's one strategy.

Indigenous Kinship Systems

On the use of water cannons and dogs on NoDAPL water protectors
November 25, 2016

They ripped water protectors' flesh
with dogs made into a weapon

our horse kin carried them to safety

They stopped an elder's heart
with oil made into a weapon

our human kin's hands restarted it

They burned water protectors' skin
with air made into a weapon

our mineral and water kin diluted it

They soaked and froze protectors
with water made into a weapon

oil kin coats and shared warmth staved it off

They marched against protectors
with humans made into a weapon

our human kin bodies stood against it

Our kin have been made their weapons
but our kin-ship will be their undoing

Ritual for Emptiness

ars poetica absentia

Close the empty notebook, the blank document
Pet the cat, refill the birdfeeder
Water the plants, breathe in the smell as the drops hit potted earth
Tidy the pantry, put the laundry in the dryer
Go for a walk, marvel at the architecture of hollow seed husks
Read a poem, a book of poems, an essay about poetry
Paint my toenails but not my fingers
Make a list of my current favorite words: *stridulation, besotted, inflorescence,*
    glaucus
Distract myself with thoughts that will not be put to paper, briefly fall asleep
Pull up drafts of unfinished poems, re-arrange the lines, substitute one word
    for another
Close the file without saving the changes
Lie down in the middle of the floor, the yard, the field of dry grasses
Pray that my words are perennial, that they are just lying dormant, waiting
For the right combination of sun and rain to resurface
Because I do not know where to find more seeds

switch physics

after Jericho Brown, "Prayer of the Backhanded"

"Go pick out a switch. And if it breaks, *I'll* pick one out"

I was only four or five the first
time I was given this punishment
(I do not remember the crime)
the bigger task was clear, but not
the latter threat, so, to avoid breakage
I cut off a thin green branch so flexible it
could have been bent into a circle

I learned first the physics of
thinness and elasticity that allows
a tree to become a whip,[1] then that of
how sound is made when something both
firm and pliable cuts through the air[2]
and, finally, a third when its momentum
meets a solid object[3] covered in soft flesh

I was learning, too, the alchemy
of transformation. Belt, wooden spoon,
sandal, tree branch. Anything can be rendered
into a source of pain, of fear, even the hands
we were supposed to reach for
when crossing the street

---

1. $D = Cd * A * 0.5 * r * V^2$
2. $u2=(\varkappa s\varrho)-1$
3. $F = dp/dt$

Truth & Reconciliation

on the acquittal of Gerald Stanley
February 9, 2018

The truth
about reconciliation
is that
while colonialism
reaches out
one hand to
shake in the guise
of acknowledgment
healing
restitution
its other hand
never puts down
the gun

Teachings of Moss

Today I attended talks
by a panel of sidewalk mosses
They said surviving
in places not meant for us
sometimes looks like fitting in
but that our bodies can also
make those barriers visible
sometimes it means making these
spaces a little bit more comfortable
for the next generations
whose roots will
be strong enough to tear it all
down from the ground up
and sometimes it means being
willing to be turned over ourselves
in the process. Becoming a part
of something new
                    mulch,
                    nutrients,
                    webbing for fungal networks
We do not need to fight for the barren
structures around us just because
we have never had the chance
to taste deep soil

Prophesies

Our prophesies are beaded into medallions
woven with cane strips into diamond patterns
coiled into baskets small enough to
be held in the palm of one hand

I can feel them watching
but there are no apologies
in my movements

Each step a dance calling worlds into being
with hips grown rounder for each new
role I am called to hold
wider for each lover pressed against them
perfectly formed to give birth
to new social movements

How many times have they
set fire to us
pressed us with stones
and sunk us to the murky lake bottoms
but they cannot drown me

I am from the fresh waters of Oklahoma
they would only be sending me
home

England Collect s

England's museum collections were announced as having been stolen

Eulogy for a Fellow Rover

on NASA's declaration of the Opportunity rover as dead
February 13, 2019

I have often
thought of you
seeing more of myself
in a robot
33 million miles away
than the people around me
as we each wander alone
on a planet unable to
shake its connection to war
making home
in some alien place
on missions we were
never meant to
return from
I found solace
in our shared experience
of surviving in hostile
climates long beyond
anyone's expectations
moving between
red dirt below
and the constellations
above

In the Glossary of Colonialism

Let's not forget
that *Raphus cucullatus* "dodo,"
has come to mean:
    "dull," "slow," "easily-caught," "defenseless"
having evolved in a
place with no significant predators
they did not know to fear the Dutch when they arrived
    Imagine interpreting
no propensity for violence
no expectation of it
as *less* sophisticated, *less* intelligent
    Imagine reading
the inability to defend oneself
it as an invitation for violence
    Imagine being so sure you were
right, you made a joke
about it for the next 300 years

Poison Ivy Medicine

Some Elders say everything
has something to teach us
even those who carry poison ivy medicine
you sit next to them at the stomp dance or brush
by them in the baked goods aisle
it does not hit for hours, sometimes days
gossip that itches
secrets that ooze and travel past trusted ears
words that dry and crust into welts drawing scandalized
looks over hymnals and napkins darkened
by fried chicken grease
if all medicine has a purpose
then theirs teaches us to walk carefully
through social woods
strip and wash clean after difficult
conversational hikes
and to take care not to transfer the oils of
ill will onto others

Public/Science

Q: When did it become illegal to kill Native Americans? (Reddit)

A: American Indian and Alaska Native (AI/AN) individuals are more likely to die than other groups, there are other important unmeasured factors that contribute to this inequity. This will be an important direction for future research.

—*Nature*, 2023

Anadromous

There are fish
who swim headfirst
against the current
to re-immerse themselves
in the tributaries of
    history
who leap over
waterfalls
not for war or glory
or even safety
but to lay groundwork
for the next
    generation
who journey
in the opposite
direction of what everyone
says is the natural
    course of things
who prove that
fish can fly
that the delineations
between salt and fresh water
are not as tidy as some
might believe and
that the drive of
even the greatest rivers
toward the sea is
    surmountable
who push forward
even when—
especially when—
the future is as fragile as
    a cluster of eggs

Madstone

on the 35th anniversary of the designation
of the Tar Creek, OK, Superfund Site
September 8, 2018

We have plunged
the madstone in
too deep
too many times
but still it turns the
warm milk green
It can pull out a rabid bite
but can't seem to draw
this venom
the doctor said
it has already
soaked into our bones
Beware the mutants
with our cement
and coal-lined lungs
oil in our marrow
lead in our blood
We are all dying
but the ones that live
will be stronger than
anyone imagined
Someone always survives
and their resistant
cells will let them
drink these waters unscathed
the way our ancestors
grew immune
to cavalry bullets

Like the wolves and bears
at Chernobyl
this will be a land
where only mutants
can live and maybe then
we will finally
be free

origami paper

no matter how far
I unfold myself
what new shapes I become
the old creases remain
I am softer
        more fragile
at those places
that still tug
to return to old
configurations

Cicada (up)Rising

17 years after you thought you had buried us
breathed sighs of relief against the
silent reprieve from our songs
we will swarm the ground you renamed after
your own kind. The shells we climb out of
are less hollow than the art you
tried to steal from us and claim as your own
We will set fire to our eyes and
force blood into unfurling wings in the
dead of night so you will not
see us coming. Our cadence will
call out the dawn of our resurgence
We are still here

Etymological Kin

Pomegranate and *grenade*
etymological kin from
the lineage of blood red
from shard and seed from
some moment when some
man held a palm-sized womb and
imagined explosions imagined
red running down chins down
legs down blown off limbs
red the color of winter months
spent underground spent
eating shrapnel

Bodies of Water

You are a deep sea
I could slip into
and never leave
take back my selkie skin
at the first temptation of wetness
glide my hands across
sun-warmed ripples
so slick as I move between
your banks, a current
tracing patterns
around time-smoothed rocks
swimming ancient rituals
of ebb and flow

Nearby Constellations

I.

The tree canopy creates a second sky and
fireflies make nearby constellations against it
a tangible heaven
of ever-moving lights drawn
by some unseen gravitational pull
leave it to a bullfrog to disrupt the cosmos
because no one told him
you shouldn't eat stars

II.

Physicists say that entangled particles
are connected no matter how far apart in space and time
they are separated
so maybe homesickness
is just the sensation of parts of us
already always dancing with the places and people
we love but cannot touch
across these distances the world
stretches out between us

Winter Bare

Bare winter limbs
expose

the structures of
our homes

give us time to
rebuild
our nests

pluck out
the newspaper strips
and baling twine
that formed
their shapes

when the grass was
sparse

when we spun dread into
string and
wove fear into
coils
mortared anger into
the cracks in the
walls

it got us
through
in a pinch
but it
will not be
enough

to sustain us in the
years
to come

the bitter cold
reminds
us
to hold each other
close

keep our axes
sharp

and some extra
flesh
on our bones

gives us time
for knotting
love into rugs
to warm
detention cell floors
and resistance camp
tarps

tattoo medicine
plants onto
skin
and keep our favorite
animal-kin
alive in stories

for future
generations
who
may never see them
anywhere
else

Volunteer Trees

remind us
    these lands used to be forests

offer us gifts of
    mulberries and prophesies of maple syrup

promise
    housing for squirrel
          chickadee
          cicada

try to teach us
    that deep roots hold back flood waters
                    drought soil

show us
    decolonization is a rhizome
                a seed
                a forest
                 that is allowed to grow where its ancestors once stood

    one tree at a time

If Quiroga Wrote Science Fiction

March 29, 2024

It might have looked like a
middle-aged woman in the
middle of a large room
carefully cradling a thousand-year-old
cranium in her hands for
the process of repatriation
while on the other side
of a low wall a robot
newly made by
university engineers
develops its motor skills
by learning to ring a bell
DING!

Seeing
sunflowers

a cultivation poem

sunflower—

sunflower

sunflower

sunflower.

sunflowers

sunflowers,

sunflower

sunflowers

sunflower

sunflower

—*Nature*, 2004

Welcome to the Indigenous Languages Slipstream

Welcome to the Indigenous languages slipstream
I imagine this is all a little disorienting—
In your universe our languages might as well
be wearing invisibility cloaks
because the only place you look for them
    is the past
        in a museum, and archive
            on a wax cylinder
In your universe you carved our languages
small enough to keep them in your pocket
to put them on your keychains and hand down to your
academic children like the good silverware
    only to be taken out
        on special occasions
            never for general use
You can't see what is all around you
because your language doesn't have a word for *Indian*
in the present tense

But look around you
    in *this* universe our languages
        are *everywhere*
Native movies don't star Kevin Costner here
(but they still star Tantoo Cardinal and Wes Studi)
Digital Indians speak Iñupiaq and Kanyen'kéha on
PS5s, memes circulate over social media
in Ararahih'uripih and Anishinaabemowin, and
the latest film in the Predator franchise can be watched
in Nʉmʉ Tekwapʉ̱ audio and subtitles
Robots speak Chikashshanompa' here

and so do the dogs, but especially
our children, our adults, and our Elders

Please keep your hands inside the vehicle at all times

Stages of an Impending Storm

storm watch

all of the ingredients for a disaster are present. someone who has been through a storm before may always be scanning for this moment, even if unconsciously. stay close to home with an eye on the horizon.

horizon

storm clouds may be visible from miles away, always inching closer. the increasing pressure and temperature shifts may be perceptible in your joints and on the back of your neck.

storm warning

a storm has been sighted in your area. this is when the sirens go off. locate your loved ones and take cover. animals that are too large to be brought inside should be turned loose to find their own safety.

wall cloud

few things are as chilling as the sight of these dark grey-green clouds in wall formation. this is technically not the storm, but its foundation, blocking out the sky. actual tornadoes are incredibly loud, but the air around wall clouds is notably silent as everything is holding its breath in wait.

tornado

debris accounts for the most casualties and injuries from a tornado. while the storm itself has a narrower, highly destructive path, it can weaponize anything in its vicinity in a much broader swath.

aftermath

long after a tornado wears itself out, its effects will still be visible on the landscape. things scattered will be discovered for years to come miles away from where they were picked up. a tree blown over will never grow tall again but animals may eventually build nests in its upturned roots.

Poem for a friend having a long week

In the arena of linguistics that studies how some sound patterns, phonesthemes, carry meaning, /gr-/ is associated with a bad mood. Did you know that *grouchy* started out as slang among US college students in the late 1800s? But *grouch* is much older. As a verb meaning "to grumble or complain" it dates at least as far back as 1200 AD. *Grumble,* now that's another great "gr" word. So are *grizzle, grimace, grind, grim, growl, grating, grey, gripe, grumpy,* and *gruff.*

Come to think of it, so are *grief* and *grieving*—maybe that's where this all started. Their root can be found in the distant ancestor of English over 12,000 years ago. These grafts of anger, of loss, still appearing, uninvited, like a piece of gravel that suddenly turns up in your shoe.

Nita' Oka' Iksa' (water bear clan)

on the launch of SpaceX rocket carrying 20,000 tardigrades to the International Space Station to be used in research
June 3, 2021

I.

This is a ceremony to recognize kin.

II.

Nanta chilholhchifo?

Saholhchifoat Shokhoshi' okchamali loposhki' "moss piglet"
Ishnowa' yáppalli "tardigrade"
Nita' oka "water bear"

Hattak api'ma' chiya?

i̱i

III.

We should have known you were Indigenous
by how often they've tried to kill
you. Froze you then boiled you alive.
Exposed you to radiation and
shot you into space just to see
if you'd die in its vacuum.

We knew you were Indigenous when you

didn't. Released all your moisture
and went quiet. Waited until
they weren't looking and revived
at the touch of water. Like us
you are impossible to kill. Unwilling
to remain dormant.

Take your place under the arbors
and dance with us alongside
Kowimihlha', *Shawi'*, *Nani'*, *Fani'*,
Nashoba', *Kowishto' Losa'*, and
Issi' Ishtaaoncholoi'. You who have
always been here alongside us.
Unconquerable.

Falammi Fochik (The North Star)

I.

If you are lost (in the Northern Hemisphere)
    look to the North Star to guide you

If you do not know which one is the North Star, you
    can find it in the handle of the Little Dipper

If you do not know where the Little Dipper is, find
    the Big Dipper and look in the direction
    of the scoop

If you do not know how to find the Big Dipper, its
    location depends on the time of year,
    the hour of night,
    and where you are standing

So if you are lost (in any hemisphere)
    it may be easier to remember where you have been
    and where you were trying to go, and hope
    that you are still somewhere in the middle

II.

In winter, the night sky points farthest from the Milky Way, leaving other stars more visible. Orion and Taurus leap out against the expanse of space. It is the hardest time of year to find the North Star.

> that is all just a long-winded way to say
> that I have been feeling lost
> that I looked up to the stars to guide me
>   and not finding the ones I was taught to follow
>   went back inside to look in books
>   there, surrounded by the
>   *New General Catalogue of Nebulae and Clusters of Stars*,
>   celestial charts full of women in the shape of monsters,
>   and astrological compendiums, I realized
> that none of them tell you where you are going only
> that our positions are relational
>   and asking the wrong questions
>   means finding the wrong answers but
>   sometimes the right ones too like
>   it is not where we are going, but
> that we are surrounded by stars

III.

The North Star is a yellow supergiant
in a triple-star system
distance and the narrow vision of former fish
means our naked eyes see only one
star   where a stellar nexus exists
or is it the myopia of man
that creates hierarchy
even among astronomical objects

What is the point of a telescope
if not to
show us that
a star shines brightest
in the context of other
stars in the pull of celestial bodies
holding themselves in place
by holding a place
for each other
in luminous configurations
of stardust

Still Trying to Get the Hands Right

I.

Right now the easiest way to tell if an image or video is generated by AI is to look at the hands. Too many fingers or too few, anywhere between ten and three, or oddly arranged. Sometimes two left hands or two of the right. I love just how human this is. Hands are hard to draw. So many curves and jointed articulations. Twenty-seven bones in each one makes it very easy to get the angle and length wrong. At least AI is honest about where it is in the learning process. I used to hide hands in pictures rather than draw them poorly. Like these programs, I just didn't have a full grasp of the anatomy.

II.

For the benefit of white medicine and science the skeletonized remains of individuals from the Indian subcontinent have been trafficked for use as anatomical references by the millions. On my campus one of these individuals, articulated with screws, bolts, and wires, has—at some unknown point in the past—had a different person's hands attached to his wrists in place of his own. And I don't know whether it would be kindness or violence to remove them. Whether sameness or wholeness would have been more important to these two people. Or what it would mean to sever such a literal connection. After all one of them has been holding the other's hands for decades.

III.

In October I got my fingers tattooed the way Chickasaw people used to before Christian soldier conquistadors forced the practice from us. My *inchọwa* are lines and dots above the two lower phalangeal joints. Some of the folks back home say that one of the reasons that we learn our language is so we can speak to the Ancestors when we join them at our death. And the same for our tattoos—that they might recognize us as kin by our shared markings. But until then, in my work handling what remains of the Ancestors' corporeal forms during the processes of repatriation and reburial, I am also hopeful that these symbols in ink might make me feel familiar to them in the moments and points of contact between us. Between palm, finger, wrist, and bone.

Diary of a Sunflower

I have spent my days
turning again and again
toward warmth
inviting friends and even
strangers to dance across my flesh
feeling myself grow
thicker
rounder
heavier
with their offerings
old promiscuities create
possibilities for new ones
what I offer has changed
and so have the faces
of my visitors
but not my joy in receiving them
this new abundance
pulls my gaze toward earth
the promises of rain-moistened soil
and the view of places I
might sink into and call myself
home

Acknowledgments

"Apocalypse Journals" was first published in *Resist Much/Obey Little: Inaugural Poems to the Resistance* (Dispatches Editions, 2017).

"Life and Limb" was first published in the *West Trestle Review* (September 2020).

"Over a Barrel" was first published in *Resist Much/Obey Little: Inaugural Poems to the Resistance* (Dispatches Editions, 2017).

"Pulse" was first published in *Gathering in the Glittering Field: An Anthology of Two-Spirit and Indigiqueer Poetry* (Litmus Press, 2026).

"Honor Song for Tulsa" was first published in the *West Trestle Review* (November, 2021).

"How the Oak Tree Came to Be" was first published in *Meridians: Feminism, Race, transnationalism* (24, no. 1, 2025), and was reprinted in *Arnoldia: The Nature of Trees.* (82, no. 3, Sept. 2025) and in the *Gathering in the Glittering Field: An Anthology of Two-Spirit and Indigiqueer Poetry* (Litmus Press, 2026).

"Teachings of Moss" was first published by *Pandemic Poem a Day* (San Francisco Public Library, July 28, 2020).

"Indigenous Kinship Systems" was first published by *Broadsided*, February 10, 2017, and was reprinted in *Resist Much/Obey Little: Inaugural Poems to the Resistance* (Dispatches Editions. 2017).

"Anadromous" was first published in *Humana Obscura* (Spring/Summer Issue, 2022).

"Nearby Constellations" was first published under the title "Home" in *Nomadic* (3rd quarter, 2020).

"Welcome to the Indigenous Languages Slipstream" was first published in the *American Indian*

Culture and Research Journal, Special Issue on Indigenous Languages in Unexpected Places, (48, no. 1 2025).

"Diary of a Sunflower" was first published in *ALOCASIA* (Issue 14, Summer 2025).

With immense thanks to the team at Michigan State University Press and especially to Jill Doerfler for stewarding a series I'm truly honored to be published in.

To Antoinette, Siobhan, Krystal, Randyn, and Kim who not only read my poems with generosity, but fill my life with the poetry of sunflowers, molasses cookies, books, tattoos, walks in the sun and the rain, and Olive Garden breadsticks. "Thank you" doesn't cover it, but it will have to do.

To my family and friends (and the many places those two overlap) thanks for keeping my days full of stories.

To my incredible students, I am grateful for everything I learn from you every day and I can't wait to read *your* books/articles/poems.

To my colleagues in AIS and on Nevada St., for all the ways we persist, resist, and find joy under compression, erasure, and exclusion.

To Cass, all journeys need a map, a compass, and a guiding star, thank you for helping me find mine.

To Sophie, McDuff, Drizzt, and Dax, thanks for all the cuddles and making sure I never have to write alone.

To Laura, *sachonkash*, as always, this book is for you.

To the Ancestors, moss, earthworms, cicadas, tardigrades, and constellations of stars, thank you for all the ways you remind me to look up and down, zoom in and out, and remember the value of softness.

AMERICAN INDIAN STUDIES SERIES

Aazheyaadizi: *Worldview, Language, and the Logics of Decolonization*, Mark D. Freeland | 978-1-61186-380-2

As Sacred to Us: Simon Pokagon's Birch Bark Stories in Their Contexts, edited by Blaire Morseau | 978-1-61186-462-5

Bawaajimo*: A Dialect of Dreams in Anishinaabe Language and Literature*, Margaret Noodin | 978-1-61186-105-1

Centering Anishinaabeg Studies: Understanding the World through Stories, edited by Jill Doerfler, Niigaanwewidam James Sinclair, and Heidi Kiiwetinepinesiik Stark | 978-1-61186-067-2

Curator of Ephemera at the New Museum for Archaic Media, Heid E. Erdrich | 978-1-61186-246-1

Document of Expectations, Devon Abbott Mihesuah | 978-1-61186-011-5

Dragonfly Dance, Denise K. Lajimodiere | 978-0-87013-982-6

Encountering the Sovereign Other: Indigenous Science Fiction, Miriam C. Brown Spiers | 978-1-61186-405-2

Facing the Future: The Indian Child Welfare Act at 30, edited by Matthew L. M. Fletcher, Wenona T. Singel, and Kathryn E. Fort | 978-0-87013-860-7

Famine Pots: The Choctaw–Irish Gift Exchange, 1847–Present, edited by LeAnne Howe and Padraig Kirwan | 978-1-61186-369-7

Follow the Blackbirds, Gwen Nell Westerman | 978-1-61186-092-4

Gambling on Authenticity: Gaming, the Noble Savage, and the Not-So-New Indian, edited by Becca Gercken and Julie Pelletier | 978-1-61186-256-0

Indian Country: Telling a Story in a Digital Age, Victoria L. LaPoe and Benjamin Rex LaPoe II | 978-1-61186-226-3

The Indian Who Bombed Berlin and Other Stories, Ralph Salisbury | 978-0-87013-847-8

Indigenizing Philosophy through the Land: A Trickster Methodology for Decolonizing Environmental Ethics and Indigenous Futures, Brian Burkhart | 978-1-61186-330-7

Indigenous Journeys, Transatlantic Perspectives: Relational Worlds in Contemporary Native American Literature, Anna M. Brígido-Corachán | 978-1-61186-469-4

Indigenous Poetics, edited by Inés Hernández-Ávila and Molly McGlennen | 978-1-61186-526-4

Louise Erdrich's Justice Trilogy: Cultural and Critical Contexts, edited by Connie A. Jacobs and Nancy J. Peterson | 978-1-61186-403-8

Masculindians: Conversations about Indigenous Manhood, edited by Sam McKegney | 978-1-61186-129-7

Mediating Indianness, edited by Cathy Covell Waegner | 978-1-61186-151-8

The Murder of Joe White: Ojibwe Leadership and Colonialism in Wisconsin, Erik M. Redix | 978-1-61186-145-7

National Monuments, Heid E. Erdrich | 978-0-87013-848-5

Ogimawkwe Mitigwaki (Queen of the Woods), Simon Pokagon | 978-0-87013-987-1

Ottawa Stories from the Springs: Anishinaabe dibaadjimowinan wodi gaa binjibaamigak wodi mookodjiwong e zhinikaadek, translated and edited by Howard Webkamigad | 978-1-61186-137-2

Picturing Worlds: Visuality and Visual Sovereignty in Contemporary Anishinaabe Literature, David Stirrup | 978-1-61186-352-9

Plain of Jars and Other Stories, Geary Hobson | 978-0-87013-998-7

Sacred Wilderness, Susan Power | 978-1-61186-111-2

Seeing Red—Hollywood's Pixeled Skins: American Indians and Film, edited by LeAnne Howe, Harvey Markowitz, and Denise K. Cummings | 978-1-61186-081-8

Self-Determined Stories: The Indigenous Reinvention of Young Adult Literature, Mandy Suhr-Sytsma | 978-1-61186-298-0

Shedding Skins: Four Sioux Poets, edited by Adrian C. Louis | 978-0-87013-823-2

Sounding Thunder: The Stories of Francis Pegahmagabow, Brian D. McInnes | 978-1-61186-225-6

Stick Houses: Stories, Matthew L. M. Fletcher | 978-1-61186-522-6

Stories for a Lost Child, Carter Meland | 978-1-61186-244-7

Stories through Theories/Theories through Stories: North American Indian Writing, Storytelling, and Critique, edited by Gordon D. Henry Jr., Nieves Pascual Soler, and Silvia Martinez-Falquina | 978-0-87013-841-6

That Guy Wolf Dancing, Elizabeth Cook-Lynn | 978-1-61186-138-9

Those Who Belong: Identity, Family, Blood, and Citizenship among the White Earth Anishinaabeg, Jill Doerfler | 978-1-61186-169-3

Visualities: Perspectives on Contemporary American Indian Film and Art, edited by Denise K. Cummings | 978-0-87013-999-4

Visualities 2: More Perspectives on Contemporary American Indian Film and Art, edited by Denise K. Cummings | 978-1-61186-319-2

Writing Home: Indigenous Narratives of Resistance, Michael D. Wilson | 978-0-87013-818-8